ORCHID CAR

Everything You Need To Know About Orchid. How To Water, Fertilize And Take Proper Care Of Them.

ROBERT EDWARD

Table of Contents

CHAPTER ONE 3
   INTRODUCTION 3
CHAPTER TWO 5
   HOW TO WATER ORCHIDS 5
CHAPTER THREE 9
   HOW TO SELECT YOUR ORCHIDS 9
CHAPTER FOUR 13
   HOW TO FERTILIZE ORCHIDS 13
CHAPTER FIVE 17
   ORCHIDS HUMIDITY 17
CHAPTER SIX 21
   TYPES OF ORCHIDS SPECIES AND WAYS TO TAKE GOOD CARE OF THEM 21
THE END 36

CHAPTER ONE

INTRODUCTION

Orchids have recognition for being hard-to-grow houseplants. Sure, they'll require specialized potting blend and a positive quantity of water to thrive, however this massive, diverse institution of plant life consists of many species that are clean to grow interior. And in return to your efforts to offer what they need, they'll praise you with their distinctive-searching vegetation for years to come. That will help you benefit self assurance being concerned for those beautiful flowering plants; we rounded up a number of our quality suggestions for maintaining them happy and healthy, which include a way to water orchids, how to fertilize them, and what potting mix to use.

CHAPTER TWO

HOW TO WATER ORCHIDS

The maximum not unusual cause of dying for orchids (and most houseplants) is normally overwatering. Instead of watering your plants on a strict schedule (every other day, or once a week, for example), take note of your orchid's desires and how much water it makes use of. This may vary based at the humidity, mild, air motion, and potting blend its roots are growing in.

The easy solution for while to water maximum orchids (inclusive of Phalaenopsis and Cattleya) is simply before they pass dry. It could be every few days, or even each couple of weeks relying on the orchid species and the environment in your property. The potting medium you use plays a critical position in how a whole lot water your orchid wishes—bark dries out fast, even as moss soaks up water and holds onto it for a long term.

To tell if it is time for a watering, stick your finger in the potting mix, then pull it out and rub your palms together. You ought to easily be able to feel if there is any moisture. If you don't experience any, it is time to water your orchid, and in case your fingers feel moist, take a look at once more any other day. Over time, you'll start to develop an experience of ways often your orchid usually needs water, and the way situations like seasonal changes can affect the frequency. You will additionally start to increase a "experience" for the way mild the pot receives whilst the bark or moss is dry, that is any other available manner to tell if your orchid desires a drink.

Watering is as easy as pouring water into the potting mix, and letting any excess drain thru the bottom. Just make certain you put your orchid in a field that has a drainage hole. it is a lot more hard to water plant life in packing containers without drainage due to the fact the water can acquire at the bottom, so if your pot does not have a hole (or some), bear in mind repotting or drilling one yourself.

CHAPTER THREE

HOW TO SELECT YOUR ORCHIDS

Potting blend plays a large function in how frequently you need to water orchids. Generally, orchids are potted in either sphagnum moss or bark chips, which both paintings properly but want barely one of a kind cares. Moss acts like a sponge, soaking up water and taking a long term to dry out. because it'll hang on to moisture for a while, you can wait longer among watering, however moss is also less forgiving if you overwater your orchid. Bark doesn't preserve lot water and drains quick, which makes it an amazing choice for orchids like Phalaenopsis and Cattleya that want to dry out between watering.

Different orchids such as lady's slipper and nun's orchid like more dampness, and could do better in case you don't let them dry out. Moss is a superb preference for those species as it'll deliver them with moisture for an extended period of time between watering. you can additionally grow these water-loving orchids in first-class-textured bark, but it nonetheless might not hang on to moisture so long as moss, so that you'll have to water them more frequently.

Your potting fabric will finally start to decompose, especially bark. You must repot your orchids in new bark each year or, as it won't drain as fast as it decomposes. Dispose of the orchid from the antique bark (which you may toss for your compost pile!), and clip off the dead roots. You have to be capable of spot any useless roots right away—they'll be darkish and contracted, in comparison to the firm, light-colored wholesome roots. Area the orchid returned inside the pot (or repot it) and fill up with new bark.

CHAPTER FOUR

HOW TO FERTILIZE ORCHIDS

The yank Orchid Society recommends feeding your plant life regularly with a 20-20-20 fertilizer with little to no urea. Another advice is to fertilize with sector-electricity, water-soluble fertilizer every time you water your plant. Which means use simply ¼ of the amount that the label recommends, and mix it with water. You may deliver this aggregate to your orchid on a weekly basis (though it's better to under-fertilize than over-fertilize). Additionally, make sure the potting mix is a touch damp earlier than fertilizing due to the fact it could burn the roots if they are completely dry.

How tons light Orchids need

From a plant's angle, houses generally have dim mild, so that you'll normally have better good fortune with orchid types that tolerate low mild tiers. East-dealing with windowsills are excellent spots for orchids; an unscreened south-going through window may be a touch too brilliant and warm, but a sheer curtain can add just the right amount of filtering. You may also set the orchid lower back from the window through some ft so it's no longer constantly in sturdy oblique mild.

West-going through home windows are commonly too hot for orchids, however with a few filtering (a sheer curtain again), you may occasionally cause them to work. We wouldn't propose attempt a north-facing window, because they may be generally just too dim for orchids to be successful.

Your orchid would not need to be glued to the identical spot even though! In case you want to apply a blooming orchid as a table centerpiece or display somewhere aside from a windowsill, there may be no damage in shifting it. Just take it returned to its spot by the window as soon as it's accomplished blooming.

CHAPTER FIVE

ORCHIDS HUMIDITY

Most orchids are tropical flowers, but that doesn't imply they need rain forest humidity to grow in your property. The dry environment of an air-conditioned home may be tough though, which is why a day by day mist, or putting your orchids on a wet mattress of gravel can assist create the humidity they crave. If making a decision to apply gravel, simply make sure the pot is sitting on pinnacle of the rocks, no longer nestled in them. in any other case, moisture can seep into the pot and drown the roots through the years.

Orchids might have extraordinary desires as compared to most of your flowers, however if you may grasp the fundamentals in their care, they can be easy-care houseplants too. Given that they are precise, you can display them in fun ways too, like developing placing planters to expose off their blooms. If you haven't attempted growing an orchid earlier than, stick to something easy, like a moth orchid, before operating your manner up to fancier varieties.

More light isn't continually the answer for healthy houseplants; just like you, your flora can grow to be getting sunburned if they spend too much time soaking up the rays. you couldn't slather them up with sunscreen earlier than you place them inside the sun, but there are some matters you could do to save you leaves from getting scalded by using too many rays. usually, your vegetation are the most at hazard within the spring and summer time if making a decision to transport them outside, or in case you circulate them to a sunny window after they're used to a spot with lower light. One of the first-rate approaches to change up their region without harming them is to go approximately it steadily so they have time to get them used to a gap with more sun.

CHAPTER SIX

TYPES OF ORCHIDS SPECIES AND WAYS TO TAKE GOOD CARE OF THEM

1. Cymbidium

Mild

Filtered mild

SOIL

Medium or quality fir bark combined with peat moss or perlite

TEMPERATURE

Those orchids have varying temperature desires at some point of the 12 months. Temperatures need to fall to about 45-55°F so as to cause winter blooms. Look ahead to temperatures above 85°F, which could purpose the leaves to burn.

WATER

Water inside the morning to allow masses of moisture to empty earlier than temperatures cool. Allow the soil to dry slightly among watering to prevent sogginess. Watering amounts rely on the temperature. be sure to water much less for the duration of the winter and extra inside the summer.

FERTILIZER

Cymbidium orchids don't require a ton of extra vitamins. Including sluggish-launch fertilizer pellets to the potting soil at the start of the season is enough for appropriate results. Pick out a balanced fertilizer and use most effective when plants are actively growing.

2. Sarcochilus

LIGHT

Slight to Low light

SOIL

Medium to coarse grade treated pine bark and river pebbles

TEMPERATURE

Most sarcochilus need minimal temperatures of 40°F to bloom nicely, and cannot tolerate temperatures over 90°F. They may tolerate a mild frost with overhead protection and steady air motion.

WATER

The potting aggregate need to be constantly moist close to the roots of the plant. Be extremely cautious now not to overwater for the duration of the iciness.

FERTILIZER

Mild feeding when in lively growth is extraordinarily useful. Use a balanced water-soluble fertilizer in the course of this period.

3. Phalaenopsis

LIGHT

Medium to bright indirect light

SOIL

Properly draining potting medium like exceptional-grade orchid bark or orchid blend

TEMPERATURE

All through the day they thrive in slight temperatures among 68-85°F. At night time they'll tolerate barely cooler environments however the temperature desires to remain regular while in bloom. Cold temperatures or drafty regions can cause flowers and buds to drop.

WATER

Water as soon as per week and allow potting mix to almost dry out among watering. Do no longer let it stand in water.

FERTILIZER

Observe Phalaenopsis fertilizer at one-zone power with each different watering while orchid isn't always in bloom. Fertilizer can also be used to encourage blooming.

4. Dendrobium

MILD

Morning solar (may be direct), Afternoon coloration

SOIL

Well draining potting medium like exceptional-grade orchid bark or orchid mix

TEMPERATURE

At some stage in the day they thrive in slight temperatures among 68-85°F. At night they'll tolerate barely cooler environments, but the temperature desires to remain consistent when in bloom. Cold temperatures or drafty regions can motive plant life and buds to drop.

WATER

Water as soon as per week and allow potting blend to almost dry out between watering. Do not permit it stand in water.

FERTILIZER

Whilst your orchid is blooming, fertilizer isn't always wanted. At some stage in the summer time, upload a balanced fertilizer with each other watering. Forestall fertilizing in fall. If no new increase seems by way of January, keep in mind a excessive phosphorus fertilizer to promote blooms.

5. Cattleya

LIGHT

Morning sun (may be direct), Afternoon color

SOIL

Coarse medium which includes medium-grade fir bark

TEMPERATURE

During the day they thrive in moderate temperatures below 85°F. At night time they decide upon barely cooler environments. Occasional temperature extremes are tolerated if publicity isn't always extended.

WATER

Allow the potting medium to end up dry between watering. In nature, those plants develop in tree tops meaning they are used to drying out among rain.

FERTILIZER

High nitrogen fertilizers can be used yr-spherical at one teaspoon in step with gallon of water. Feed as soon as a month.

6. Vanda

MILD

Morning sun (can be direct), Afternoon shade

SOIL

Coarse medium such as medium-grade fir bark

TEMPERATURE

At some point of the day they thrive in slight temperatures between below 85°F. At night they decide on slightly cooler environments. Occasional temperature extremes are tolerated if exposure isn't always extended.

WATER

In nature, those plant lives grow in tree tops, wherein they often dry out between periods of rain. When watering, allow the potting medium to dry before watering again.

FERTILIZER

Excessive nitrogen fertilizers may be used all year round. Mix one teaspoon with one gallon of water, and fertilize with this aggregate once a month.

7. Paphiopedilum

LIGHT

Low light

SOIL

Medium or fine fir bark blended with peat moss or perlite

TEMPERATURE

If the plant has mottled leaves, ensure the temperature remains among 60-80°F. The extra not unusual Pahpiopedilums without mottled leaves can endure steady temperatures as little as 50°F.

WATER

Water every 5 days. Test periodically to peer if the top feels dry, and be sure not to over water.

FERTILIZER

Paphiopedilum require little fertilizing. If the plant is in bark, use excessive nitrogen fertilizer during growing season. In any other case use a balanced fertilizer every other week in half energy, and ensure to flush the fertilizer with clean water as soon as a month.

THE END